WEATHER MAKES THEM SLEEP

GARTER SNAKE HIBERNATION

by Martha London

Consultant: Beth Gambro
Reading Specialist, Yorkville, Illinois

Minneapolis, Minnesota

Teaching Tips

Before Reading

- Look at the cover of the book. Discuss the picture and the title.
- Ask readers to brainstorm a list of what they already know about garter snakes. What can they expect to see in this book?
- Go on a picture walk, looking through the pictures to discuss vocabulary and make predictions about the text.

During Reading

- Read for purpose. Encourage readers to think about garter snake hibernation as they are reading.
- Ask readers to look for the details of the book. What do garter snakes do to get ready to hibernate?
- If readers encounter an unknown word, ask them to look at the sounds in the word. Then, ask them to look at the rest of the page. Are there any clues to help them understand?

After Reading

- Encourage readers to pick a buddy and reread the book together.
- Ask readers to name one reason garter snakes sleep. Find the page that tells about this thing.
- Ask readers to write or draw something they learned about garter snake hibernation.

Credits:
Cover and title page, © Jim Maley/iStock; 3, © Michiel de Wit/Shutterstock; 5, © shanedhumphreys/iStock; 7TL, © In Stock/iStock; 7TR, © Mark Baldwin/Adobe Stock; 7BL, © Steve Healey/Shutterstock; 7BR, © Wirestock/iStock; 8-9, © Ryan H Cease/Wirestock Creators/Adobe Stock; 10-11, © Paul Roedding/Adobe Stock; 13, © Hummingbird Art/Adobe Stock; 14-15, © ChristinaPrinn/iStock; 17, © ChristinaPrinn/iStock; 18-19, © Andrew DuBois / Alamy Stock Photo/Alamy; 20-21, © Ron Rowan/Adobe Stock; 22T, © Stefan Schug/Shutterstock; 22ML, © Mike Wilhelm/Adobe Stock; 22MR, © Jean Landry/iStock; 22B, © Chris Hill/Shutterstock; 23TL, © Mickilu/iStock; 23TR, © All Canada Photos / Alamy Stock Photo/Alamy; 23BL, © vovan13/iStock; 23BR, © Fiona M. Donnelly/Shutterstock.

STATEMENT ON USAGE OF GENERATIVE ARTIFICIAL INTELLIGENCE
Bearport Publishing remains committed to publishing high-quality nonfiction books. Therefore, we restrict the use of generative AI to ensure accuracy of all text and visual components pertaining to a book's subject. See BearportPublishing.com for details.

Library of Congress Cataloging-in-Publication Data

Names: London, Martha, author. | Gambro, Beth, consultant.
Title: Garter snake hibernation / by Martha London ; consultant Beth Gambro, Reading Specialist.
Description: Minneapolis, Minnesota : Bearport Publishing Company, [2024] |
  Series: Weather makes them sleep | Includes bibliographical references
  and index.
Identifiers: LCCN 2023028923 (print) | LCCN 2023028924 (ebook) | ISBN
  9798889162254 (library binding) | ISBN 9798889162308 (paperback) | ISBN
  9798889162346 (ebook)
Subjects: LCSH: Garter snakes--Juvenile literature. | Garter
  snakes--Hibernation--Juvenile literature.
Classification: LCC QL666.O636 L66 2024 (print) | LCC QL666.O636 (ebook)
  | DDC 597.96/21565--dc23/eng/20230712
LC record available at https://lccn.loc.gov/2023028923
LC ebook record available at https://lccn.loc.gov/2023028924

Copyright © 2024 Bearport Publishing Company. All rights reserved. No part of this publication may be reproduced in whole or in part, stored in any retrieval system, or transmitted in any form or by any means, electronic, mechanical, photocopying, recording, or otherwise, without written permission from the publisher.

For more information, write to Bearport Publishing, 5357 Penn Avenue South, Minneapolis, MN 55419.

Contents

Cozy Cave 4

Snakes in Every Season 22

Glossary 23

Index 24

Read More 24

Learn More Online 24

About the Author 24

Cozy Cave

Brr!

It is getting cold outside.

A garter snake **slithers** into a cave.

Why is the snake doing that?

5

Garter snakes live in places with four **seasons**.

The weather changes during the year.

Summers are hot.

Winters are very cold.

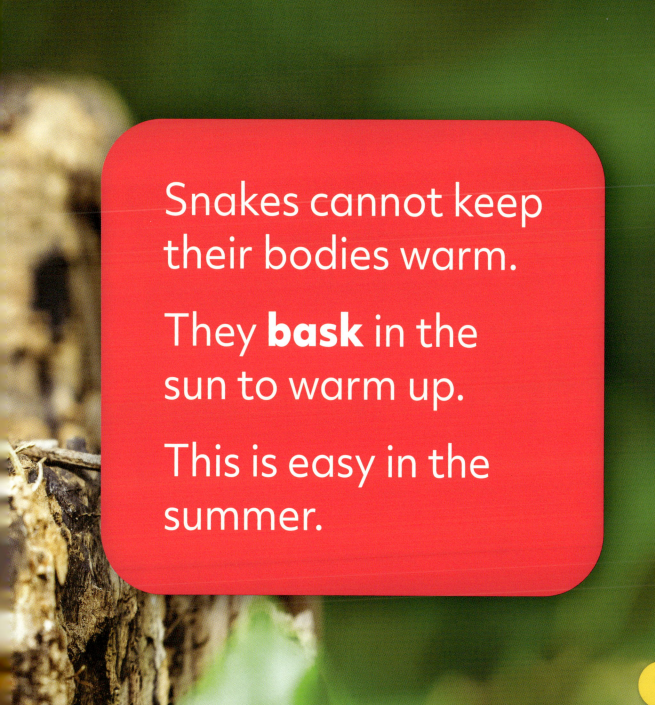

Snakes cannot keep their bodies warm.

They **bask** in the sun to warm up.

This is easy in the summer.

Weather gets colder in the fall.

Snakes can get sick if they are too cold.

Garter snakes must find a **den** for winter.

Dens keep snakes safe from the winter chill.

Some garter snakes hide in piles of wood.

Others go underground.

Many snakes use the same dens every year.

Garter snakes usually live in small groups.

But during winter, they gather in large groups.

Often, hundreds of snakes use the same den.

The snakes curl up together to share body heat.

Then, they sleep.

Garter snakes snooze for up to six months.

In the spring, the weather starts to get warmer.

It is time for the snakes to wake up.

They slither out into the sun and warm up.

Garter snakes leave their large groups.

They will do it all again next winter!

21

Snakes in Every Season

22

Glossary

bask to lie in the warmth of the sun

den a hidden place where an animal sleeps

seasons the parts of the year with different weather

slithers moves along by sliding back and forth

Index

bask 9, 22
den 10, 12, 14, 22
group 14, 20, 22
season 6, 22
sleep 16, 22
winter 6, 10, 12, 14, 20, 22

Read More

Banks, Rosie. *Why Do Animals Hibernate? (Why Do Animals Do That?).* New York: Gareth Stevens Publishing, 2024.

McDonald, Amy. *Snakes (Animals in My Yard).* Minneapolis: Bellwether Media, 2021.

Learn More Online

1. Go to **www.factsurfer.com** or scan the QR code below.
2. Enter **"Garter Snake Hibernation"** into the search box.
3. Click on the cover of this book to see a list of websites.

About the Author

Martha London loves writing about animals! She has two cats. They love to sleep in the sun.